Machines to Thrill You!

by Grace Hansen

ABDO
SEEING IS BELIEVING
Kids

abdopublishing.com

Published by Abdo Kids, a division of ABDO, PO Box 398166, Minneapolis, Minnesota 55439.

Copyright © 2015 by Abdo Consulting Group, Inc. International copyrights reserved in all countries. No part of this book may be reproduced in any form without written permission from the publisher.

Printed in the United States of America, North Mankato, Minnesota.

102014

012015

Photo Credits: AP Images, Getty Images, iStock, Shutterstock, USAF, © User:Pappnaas666 / CC-SA-3.0 p.5, © Mercier-Jones p.13, © Aeros p.15 / Rex Features

Production Contributors: Teddy Borth, Jennie Forsberg, Grace Hansen

Design Contributors: Laura Rask, Dorothy Toth

Library of Congress Control Number: 2014943700

Cataloging-in-Publication Data

Hansen, Grace.

 Machines to thrill you! / Grace Hansen.

   p. cm. -- (Seeing is believing)

ISBN 978-1-62970-732-7

Includes index.

1. Machinery--Juvenile literature. 2. Curiosities and wonders--Juvenile literature. I. Title.

629--dc23

                    2014943700

Table of Contents

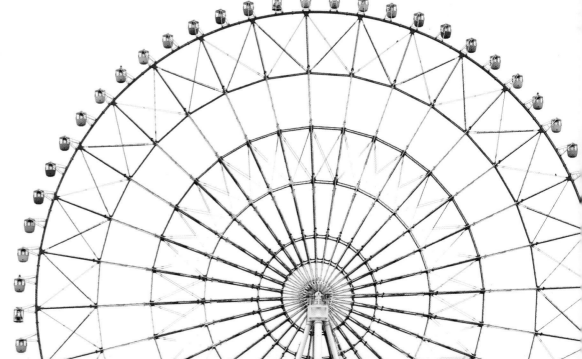

Land

The Bagger 288 is a giant **excavator**. It is longer than two football fields!

Water

The Seabreacher is a watercraft.

It moves like a dolphin.

It can go 55 miles per hour

(88.5 km/h). It can jump

15 feet (4.6 m) out of the water!

7

Hydro jet packs use water to move. Some can go 25 mph (40 km/h). They can reach heights of 30 feet (9 m).

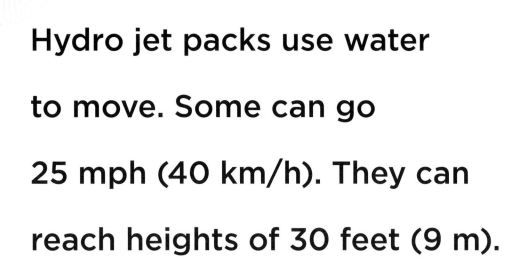

The Scubster is a personal **submarine**. It is like an underwater bike. You pedal to move it.

Land and Air

The Supercraft is a hovercraft. Hovercrafts can move over land and water.

12

13

Air

The Airship flies by being lighter than air. It uses **helium** to do this. It will be used to carry **cargo**.

14

15

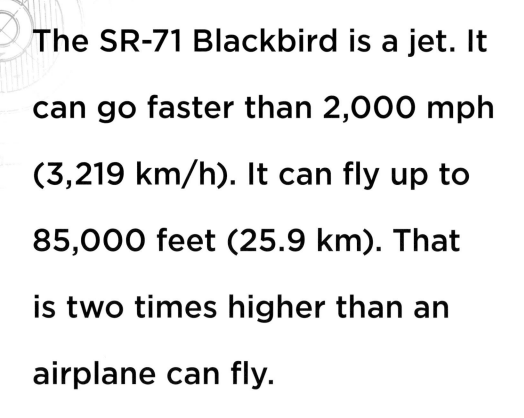

The SR-71 Blackbird is a jet. It can go faster than 2,000 mph (3,219 km/h). It can fly up to 85,000 feet (25.9 km). That is two times higher than an airplane can fly.

Tracks

The RHB X rot 9213 is a snow blower train. Large blades **rotate**. They cut through snow on the track.

Ferris Wheel

High Roller is a Ferris wheel.

It is the tallest in the world.

It is in Las Vegas, Nevada.

It is 550 feet (168 m) tall.

More Facts

- The Bagger 288 is mainly used for coal mining. It can dig up and move 240,000 tons (217,724 metric tons) of coal in one day.

- The model for the Aeroscraft Airship was just 266 feet (81 m) long. The full-scale Aeroscraft will be 400 feet (122 m) long.

- The Mercier-Jones Supercraft is the first **luxury** hovercraft. Made to perform like a high-end sports car, the Supercraft has seating for two and starts out at $75,000.

Glossary

cargo – goods carried by ship, aircraft, or motor vehicle.

excavator – a large machine for removing soil and rock.

helium – a chemical element and gas that is lighter than air.

luxury – something that is expensive and enjoyable, but not necessary.

rotate – to move in a circular motion.

submarine – a boat that can go under the water.

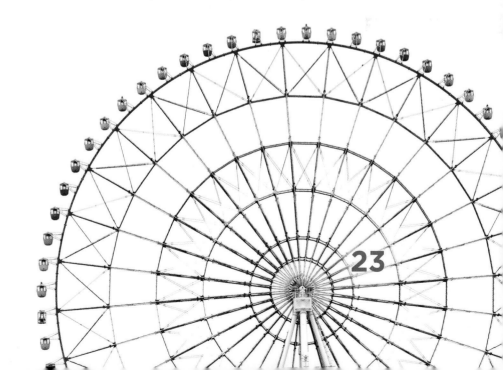

23

Index

abdokids.com

Use this code to log on to abdokids.com and access crafts, games, videos, and more!

Abdo Kids Code:
SMK7327